Drawing

for the Artistically Undiscovered

by Quentin Blake and John Cassidy

KLUTZ

KLUTZ is a kids' company staffed entirely by real human beings. We began our corporate life in 1977 in an office we shared with a Chevrolet Impala. Today we've outgrown our founding garage, but Palo Alto, California, remains Klutz galactic headquarters. For those of you who collect corporate mission statements, here's ours:
• Create wonderful things.
• Be good.
• Have fun.

Write Us
We would love to hear your comments regarding this or any of our books. We have many!

KLUTZ
455 Portage Avenue
Palo Alto, CA 94306

Book manufactured in Malaysia; pen in Austria; pencils in Germany.

Visit Us

KLUTZ.com OPEN 24 HOURS
Come on in!

ISBN 1-57054-320-8

4 1 5

Additional Copies and More Supplies
For the location of your nearest Klutz retailer, call (650) 857-0888. Should they be tragically out of stock, additional copies of this book, more pencils and pens, and the entire library of 100% certified Klutz certified books are available in our mail order catalog. See back page.

Whose Book Is This?
YOURS!

What mastery!

We've just helped around the edges with bits of technique
and encouragement. Center stage is all the white space
in the book and it's been left for you.

To get started, and since it's your book,
we'd like you to sign it.
Many times.

Marley Kirkpatrick   Samantha

Sign your name.

Marley Kirkpatrick   Samantha K

Sign your name like you were in a car with a flat on a bad road.

Marley Kirkpatrick

Sign your name with the hand you don't normally use.

Marley   &   Kirkpatrick

Sign your name as if you were
the King or Queen of England.

Marley Kirkpatrick

Sign your name in a phone booth.

3

This Is a Book on Learning How to DRAW

It's written and illustrated for anyone, particularly those who cannot reliably find the pointy end of their pencil.

Pointy end

The school of art that this book lives within is informal, a friendly, no-need-to-get-up kind of place.

The goal of the book is quite personal — to provide you with a new tool for expressing your you-ness.

The techniques it describes are a means to make you happier with your drawings. But it's not a tight set of lessons on perspective, light and shadow, and photo-realistic technique. In this book we take a whole other approach.

On the Basic Idea

Here in this book, we favor the Gung-Ho approach to art. When you're being tempted by a blank piece of paper, arm yourself with a drawing tool, think about what you're going to draw, take another moment to think about what the "essential" of it is — and then just toss that ball up and (artistically speaking) give it a good swat across the net.

If it hits — you'll have a drawing that combines wit and spontaneity with straight-to-the-heart accuracy.

And if it misses — just toss another one up, something good's bound to happen eventually.

One thing is for certain, you won't ever be able to land a booming serve with trembling hesitancy.

How Do I Criticize My Art Properly?

It's easy! On every page we've included a space ESPECIALLY for your negative comments. That's how important we think they are. Here's the space for your negative comments on this page.

On Misteakes

We don't believe in them. You'll note, in fact, that the erasers have all been painstakingly removed from our pencils. We did this ourselves, by hand, at our eraser-removal plant because you won't (can't) make any mistakes in drawing with these particular pencils. This is not to say you won't get some drawings that succeed more than others. That's our next point.

← BONUS
No Eraser!

Water soluble
BLACK pencil

5

On Success

Drawings, of course, do succeed in different ways, and in different degrees. In our book, we describe a successful drawing as one which captures (with dead-eye accuracy) something interesting or essential about the subject. This can happen by accident (often does) but you are still allowed to take full credit for it. A drawing of a monster, for example, might be quite successful by our standards, even though the details were horribly botched, as long as the ferocity of the thing was well caught, for example:

The Ferocious 5-footed Mangler

But Will I Learn How to Draw *Properly?*

Of course.

But let us make a small point at the same time. In this book, we don't spend much time on the techniques of photo-realistic art (where the art attempts to look like a photograph). This book doesn't aim to give you the skills to imitate the accurate surface of something (or someone). We're a little trickier than that, with another kind of goal.

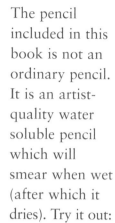

Draw a line from here...

...to here...

...to here...

...to here...

...to here...

...to here...

...and lastly, finally, concludingly, to here.

The pencil included in this book is not an ordinary pencil. It is an artist-quality water soluble pencil which will smear when wet (after which it dries). Try it out:

Make a line that is fat, skinny, straight, wiggly, each in turn. Use the point, or use the side. At the end, spit on your finger and make it into a lovely long skinny smear.

Our Goal

To give you the ability to sneak into the heart of your subject by going direct. We're not so much interested in the appearance of something, so much as the "something" itself.

What Do We Mean By That?

Think of it this way: An effective poem wastes no words on its way to the core of its subject. A successful drawing wastes no lines on the same trip. One can spend weeks on a marvelous painting of a rabbit, accurate to the tiniest detail — and yet still miss its essential rabbit-ness. And then dash off a funny little sketch in a few lines — and pin that bunny's soul to the paper.

Moon Rabbit

Drawing Jazz

If this were a piano, and not a book, these drawings would be bits of improvised jazz more than classical scales or movements. Just like jazz riffs, they're not completely free-form (you can't just pound on the keys) but they're far from rigid either. When it comes to proper rules and structure, these kinds of drawings take a middle path. Finding that path means you have to pay some dutiful attention to the "rules" (light, shadow, perspective, anatomy) but not so much as to drain away all the energy and fun, or to preclude some personal interpretation when reality is too limiting. How do you find the balance? Fool around. Find the notes that sound good and play with them in your very own funny ways.

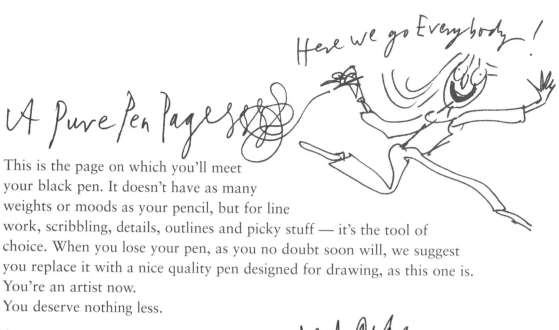

Here we go Everybody!

A Pure Pen Page

This is the page on which you'll meet
your black pen. It doesn't have as many
weights or moods as your pencil, but for line
work, scribbling, details, outlines and picky stuff — it's the tool of
choice. When you lose your pen, as you no doubt soon will, we suggest
you replace it with a nice quality pen designed for drawing, as this one is.
You're an artist now.
You deserve nothing less.

As you can see, this page is only
partially complete. We'd like you
to finish it.

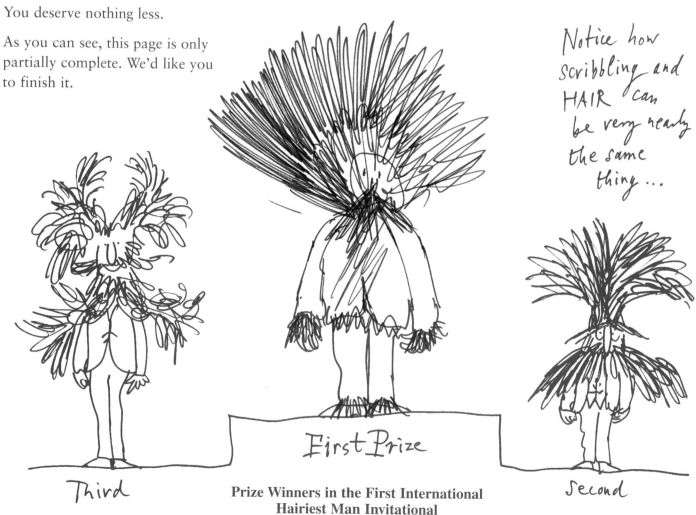

Notice how
scribbling and
HAIR can
be very nearly
the same
thing ...

Third

First Prize

Second

**Prize Winners in the First International
Hairiest Man Invitational
St. Petersberg, 1926**

How BIG Should I Draw?

Work at a comfortable — not too big, not too little — kind of scale. Try to do four or five things from your imagination or the suggestion pile, and try to fit them all right here on this page. Use your pen only.

palm-tree

hot-air-balloon

CBC

Mailbox

horseshoe

scissors

It's going to be a giraffe.

flag and flagpole

Suggestion Pile: A palm tree, hot air balloon, mailbox, horseshoe, unicycle, tennis racket, barbells, hatchet, scissors, flag and flagpole.

What is it? A microbe?

A Pure Pencil Page

This is an all-smear page. Use your water soluble black pencil, spit on your finger, and use it to smear the pencil line. Have fun. You're warming up.

Add smoke to here...

and here...

and here.

Another WET FINGER Page

add smoke to here

add smoke to here

When you lose the pencils that came with this book you will have to visit an art supply store to replace them. They are not ordinary pencils.

Where Should I Start My Drawings?

The ironclad rule about where to start your drawings is this: It varies. Generally speaking, start your drawing on the bit where you suspect it's going to be the trickiest. That way, if you get de-railed, it happens early. On the other hand, if it comes off, you're launched.

Where's the trickiest bit? Oftentimes it's centered on the drawing's "essential idea," the heart of the drawing which you usually want to think about before setting pen or pencil to paper. The drawings below are of different things (candles and people) but the essential bits are actually quite alike. And all the drawings were started with "wilting," "dumpy" or "ramrod straight" in mind from the beginning.

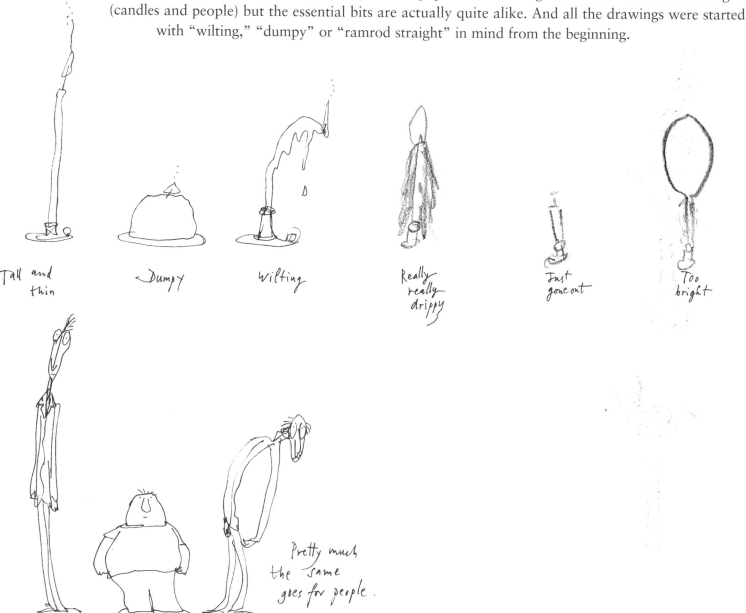

Tall and thin

Dumpy

wilting

Really really drippy

Just gone out

Too bright

Pretty much the same goes for people.

Brooms, Rakes, Mops and Dusters

We spend a lot of time in this book letting you play around with familiar shapes (like these here). How come? One, it takes the pressure off your visual memory so you can relax about unremembered shapes and details; and two, it gives you the chance to discover how much more expressive drawings can be than mere reality.

Your job here is to fill this page with brooms, rakes, mops and dusters. Make them realistic or not. It's up to you. Pull from the suggestion pile if you need ideas.

Suggestion Pile: Twisty, wilted, electrically powered, just back from the hairdresser, as designed by a committee, in a huge bucket, good for around-the-corner work, factory reject, very tall, very fat, broomerang (dual purpose).

Rain & Umbrellas

Use both pen & pencil here to add rain, clouds, and umbrellas. Rain clouds are darker than rain.
General rule about wet finger smearing: A little goes a long way.

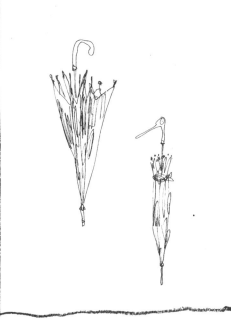

A Classic Study
of the Furled Umbrella
in Its Many Forms By

_____

Your Name Here

A Pure Pen Page

Find a cup or a glass. Set it in front of you. Fill it with pens, pencils, chopsticks, etc. Draw it. Then rearrange it and draw it again. Then, for a change of pace, rearrange it in a new cup or glass and try again. There's an untidiness to a cupful of sticks that you can best catch with a careless what-the-heck kind of approach. Keep the same cup in front of you for the next page.

A classic study of pencils, pens and brushes by _____

An Art School Exercise:
Draw Without Peeking

Try drawing the cup without looking at it (only at your hand). Then, for a change, look **only** at the cup, not your hand.

Draw your cupful of sticks *without* looking at it.

Draw your cupful of sticks *only* looking at your drawing.

Getting an Idea: *or,*
How to Think of Things to Draw

Here you are. You're sitting comfortably. On the table before you lies a sheet of clean paper, untouched and snowy white. You're equipped with a well-sharpened pencil. You're ready, armed — and, of course, absolutely baffled.

Why? Blank Page Anxiety. Your mind is mush. From the entire planet and all its contents, you can't think of a single thing to draw.

If this is your problem, do not be afraid. Absolutely everybody has it, and with absolutely every right.

You have to be prepared. You need a few tricks. You're bigger and stronger than any sheet of blank paper. Remember it's not a stage. There is no audience. Here is what we suggest to get you started. Use whichever of these tips works best for you.

- **Draw whatever's in front of you.** We favor small familiar objects. Forks, vases, books, etc.

- **Think of the category first.** Like "tools," "kitchen stuff," "hats," "red"… With your category in mind, you can pull some small, familiarly shaped objects out of it. For example: "Heavy" leads to "brick, anchor, and anvil." "Red" goes to "tomato, rose, and reindeer nose." "Curly" suggests "pretzel, vines and country roads."

- **Go alphabetical.** Don't laugh. This works very well. Or use a dictionary to make it work even better. "Acorn, airplane, ape, apple … bagel, bag, bacteria, belt … cookie, clam, cloud, comb …"

A Page to Draw Absolutely Anything You Want

We don't need THIS.

← Add the thing you draw best.

Meet Your RED Pencil

In this book you've got three colors to work with: black, red, and, of course, the white of the paper itself. Plus, there's a bonus palette inside each of the pencils since they will smear and wash through a world of pinks and grays with nothing but a wetted finger. Or for a little more control, you can use a wetted watercolor brush.

Add red to each of these drawings wherever you think you should.

Here, paint this Barn—

You've got ten minutes.

I knew you'd love it.

I think I'm blushing.

I think I've got measles!

Floor length tresses
....to here

What If the World Doesn't Like My Drawings?

The world's population, it is estimated, will soon be 8 billion people. It is difficult, with a group that large, to get everyone to agree completely on many issues. If you are concerned that not all of the world's population will appreciate all of your drawings equally, your fears are probably well-grounded. In fact, you may as well reconcile yourself to this reality right now: The reaction of the world to your art will be — inevitably — mixed. Now that that's out of the way, you should be standing in front of the essential, absolutely key question that all of this raises:

So what?

Your job is not to poll 8 billion people for their collective taste in artwork. Your job is to take your pen, pencil, brush, crayon, chalk, and greasy thumbprint — and set them to paper.

Our concluding suggestion? Draw, produce, create. Don't criticize yourself. Don't cringe when someone looks right through your drawings — and don't fly off on wings of ecstasy when someone else loves them.

You're working for yourself here.

And your Mum, of course.

On Drawing Speed

Use a civilized walking pace when you draw.

Don't agonize over your work, and don't dash through it either. Neither extreme has any special virtue.

Use a steady walking pace...

too slow and things look labored ...

too fast and they look frittery and scattered.

On the Dangers of Too Much Work

Overworking is against the rules. If you grip the pen tightly, bear down hard, push your nose into the paper and agonize over every line ... your drawings will look like hard labor. If you back off, relax, do a little sketching and stop before you think you need to, your drawings will begin to look like sparks of spontaneity and fun

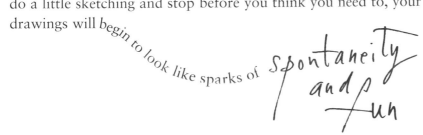

The Bucket, a Thing of Forgotten Beauty

Try drawing a few buckets. If you like, put some character into them. See suggestion pile.

pretty good eh?

with measles

with makeup

Pow!

Bucket Suggestion Pile: Try drawing buckets that are: Bucket Ordinaire, Bucket in London fog, Bucket filled with red paint, Bucket having nervous breakdown, Bucket formerly owned by Louis XIV, Bucket having fallen from great height, factory reject.

The Accident Factor

Some drawings come off. Some don't. Sometimes your first line leads naturally to the next, and that one to the next, and so on. Other times, your first line takes you right to nowhere. The difference? Leading art experts agree — it's luck. Some drawings are blessed, some aren't. But don't be alarmed. Here's a way to turn this reality to excellent use:

When a drawing works, it's your fault entirely. When it doesn't, it's not. It's the drawing's.

Your goal, of course, is to set things up so that the luck factor works for you, so that the accidents are mostly happy ones. This is quite possible, of course, and if you find yourself looking at a drawing and saying, "That's really quite nice ... [pause] How'd I do that?" then you're on the right track and the accidents are falling your way. On purpose.

Many Hammers

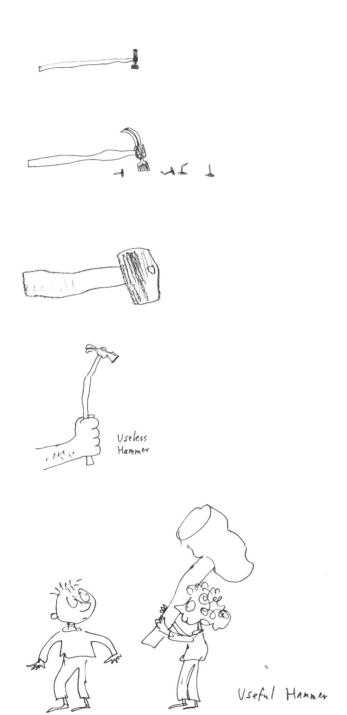

Useless Hammer

Useful Hammer

Hammer Suggestion Pile: Try drawing hammers that are: melted, fancy, double-headed, overbuilt, designer label, crossed with a pretzel, under water, battery-powered or for use in really small apartments.

Spectacles

Since it can be challenging enough simply to draw a pair of spectacles that look like the real thing, you should be quite content to limit your spectacle-drawing goals to nothing but recognizability. But if you insist on pushing yourself further, try drawing them with character. See the suggestion pile for ideas.

Suggestion Pile: Draw a pair of spectacles that have been: run over, rejected by the factory, owned by a pirate, built with wet noodles, equipped with windshield wipers, designed by a cubist, built for speed, owned by a famous actress, repaired with a safety pin, tied in a knot, worn by a little old lady, owned by someone with really bad eyes, half-built before the money ran out.

what a good idea

Cups and Pitchers

Cup Suggestion Pile: Try drawing cups or pitchers that are: tall, fat, knocked over, exhausted, over-caffeinated, for setting in cars or roller coasters, winged, leaky, realistic (sort of).

Clocks

Normal

Feeble

Hysterical

Clock Suggestion Pile: Try drawing clocks that are: off the Starship Enterprise, seen from enormous distance, previously owned by a rodeo star, muscle-bound, talking, thoughtful, very thin, very tall, very fat, speared heartlessly, one-legged, equipped with mouse ears, terribly over-built, wired to some dynamite, used as an archery target.

Candles

Candle Suggestion Pile: Try drawing candles that are: 300 watt, pretzelized, good for looking around corners, self-important, electrically powered, lazy, saying something, very tall, very fat, unusable, leaning, wearing a lamp shade, wheeled.

Drawing Things That Are Right in Front of You

When you're drawing from life — from something sitting right there in front of you — there's a problem with too much information. You are seeing more than you can ever possibly get down on paper. Putting pen to paper feels a bit like trying to catch a waterfall in a cup. A small sense of hopelessness sets in.

But don't despair. Drawings get better with time. Even yours. Afterwards, when the thing itself is gone from view, that little drawing will suddenly bloom; and you'll discover for yourself how much of a waterfall actually does fit into a cup.

Fill this space with a drawing of a few things that are around you right now.

These are the things that were right in front of me.

Drawing Things That Are <u>Not</u> Right in Front of You

Remembering how a thing looks is a very different task from drawing it, and at this stage in your artistic career you may want to limit your problems to simply the drawing bit. On the other hand, if you're eager to test your visual memory, or if you're stuck somewhere with nothing but blank walls to stare at, at least take it easy on yourself. When you're trying to draw from memory, conjure up images with simple distinctive shapes — things like flowers, dishes, tools, buildings. Or draw something from out of the kitchen. Avoid complications (bicycles are nearly impossible to figure out even when you're standing in front of one, and cars are far more difficult than you'd imagine).

MY SISTER

Drawing from Memory

A Few Potted Plants for You to Finish Drawing

It just looks dead to me.

Notice the sensitive line work.

Finish drawings. Add plants to pots.

Suggestion Pile: Overgrown, never-sprouted, receives TV, limp, lumpy, leafy, spiky, sturdy, shy, smelly, snooty, flowery, fashion-conscious, frumpy, very tall, very fat.

Portrait of the Rare but Deadly Flowering Chomp-Chomp Tree

It isn't often you see a man-eating one nowadays.

How to Get Some Perspective in Your Drawings

The artist's trick of getting a flat image to look as if it lived in space, and not just on a page, can be explored to enormous, life-consuming lengths. But for those who wish only to dabble in it, and not to soak, there is one simple truth which underlies all the complex technique: Things that are far away look smaller than things that are nearby. This is one of those facts that you already know so well it almost takes an effort to remember it (like re-discovering the location of your hands there at the end of your arms).

A large but extremely light long log →

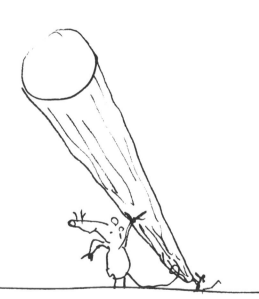

Extend this idea of "faraway things look smaller" and you soon arrive at the (unstartling) conclusion that things that are VERY far away must be completely invisible.

Which brings us to the second most basic idea in perspective drawing: the vanishing point.

Perhaps the clearest way to describe the vanishing point is this. If you are standing on a desert highway, one that's arrow straight and dead flat, the vanishing point is where the highway disappears into the distance, where the two sides of it come together at the horizon.

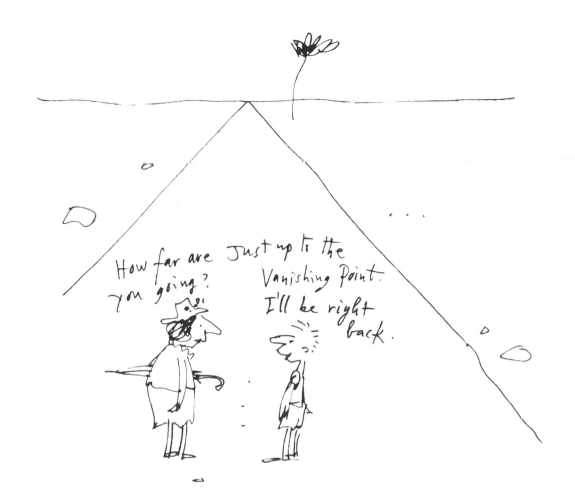

How far are you going?

Just up to the Vanishing Point. I'll be right back.

DISAPPEARING INTO THE DISTANCE

SINKING INTO THE GROUND

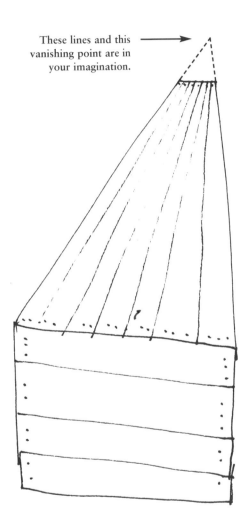

These lines and this vanishing point are in your imagination.

What's in it then?

A particularly large stuffed alligator, I believe.

Every three-dimensional object has at least one vanishing point, a place where all its going-away lines meet and disappear. When you're drawing an object with accurate perspective, you'll want to keep this vanishing point in mind. For those times when you choose not to draw desert highways or lengthy pipelines, you will have to imagine your subject's vanishing point and "draw" all the lines that reach it in your imagination.

Despite the frightening potential for difficulties in trying to get accurate perspective into your drawings, there are two bits of good news attached to all of this. One, the most basic rule, the far-away-means-smaller rule, you learned a few days after you were born. All you're doing is re-remembering it.

And two, we are not strict graders about this vanishing point rule. Like nearly all the "rules" to drawing, we do not enforce this one rigidly. As long as you know the vanishing point exists, we are happy. In any of your drawings, you may ignore it knowingly and cheerfully, or simply wave to it as you go by; in either case we will award full points.

Lovely Leafy Lane Vanishes into the Distance

A Portrait in Perspective by _____

Your Name Here

You might like to add hills in the distance. In the midground or foreground, add a few buildings or trees.

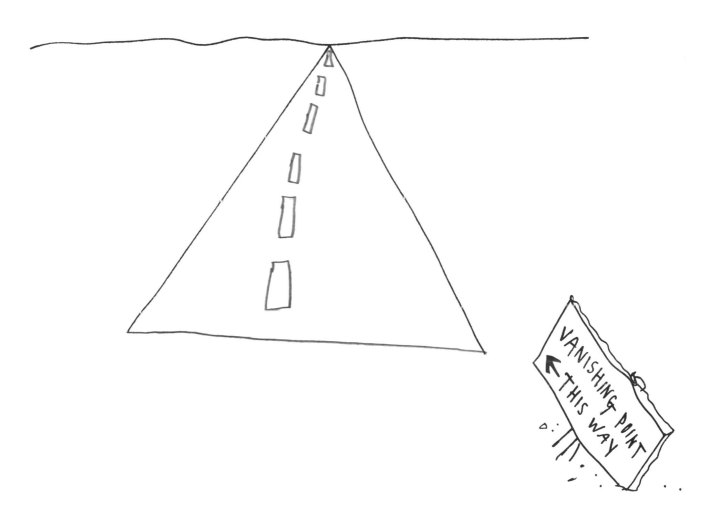

VANISHING POINT THIS WAY

The Road to Tipperary

Road disappears here

And then the road curved away into the distance, through trees and rocks and over hills and mountains.....

Foreground Freddy Turns His Back to the Road, the Hills, Some Trees, a House or Two, and His Friend, Far-Off Frank

Add road, trees, house, hills, birds; anything you can think of.

Using Light and Shadow

You can live a very long and satisfying artistic life without ever using any shading or shadows in your drawings at all. Or, you can put some shadow into everything you do. It all depends on your drawing, your eye, and the way you're feeling at that particular moment. Like most people though, you'll probably use shadow at times, and at other times — you won't.

When you do decide to add shadow, you have to ask one question: From which direction is your subject being lit ... Overhead? Underneath? From the left? From the right? Light comes from all over the place, but there is generally one main source of light, and it's this that we want to bear in mind. Often it's the sun; but for the purposes of our drawings, think of a flashlight.

The shading goes on the parts of your subject away from the light. In general, use a very light touch for shading and quit well before you think you need to. If you don't, you'll run the risk of putting what looks like an ink-blot on the unlit parts of your drawing.

Finish This One Up

Add shadow to give the crate weight. The light is shining from above. Use the side of your pencil.

Finish Up this Picture—

With the light coming from this direction

With the light coming from this direction

Shadows Can Add ...

Weight....

Realism....

Mystery....

Terror....

....or Altitude

A Shadow Practice Page

spotlight on rabbit

You do this one.

If you draw a straight line from the candle through the head to the wall you can get an idea of how tall the shadow should go.

You do this one.

42

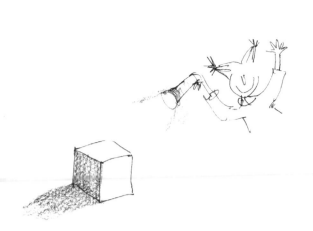

STOP!
This Page Is a Quiz

Each of these boxes is being lit by its own flashlight. Your job is to draw in the flashlight. The shadows should tell you where to put it.

← shadow

cast shadow ↓

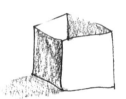

Help!

43

Using Perspective and Shadow Together

Use the watercolor pencil and a wet finger to get a nice smeary shadow. Work light and quit before you think you need to.

shade and perspective! Where will it all end?

Add flashlight and shadow.

Draw the flashlight that's lighting this crate, and then draw the shadows on it.

Barns, Bricks and  Boxes

Try drawing some kind of boxy shape. Use shadow and shading to help show weight and perspective.

Early effort at building a giraffe barn

Suggestion Pile: A barn for pythons, a barn built by beginners, a barn with 11 chimneys. A brick, a stack of bricks, a brick with wings, a brick with feet, an electric brick, a brick with a wind-up key. A plain old cardboard box, a pole vaulter's box, a box with a window, a box with big ears, a box after a great fall, a box heartlessly speared.

Using Shading to Change Flat Round Things to  Spheres

Changing a circle (like a coin) to a sphere (like an orange) is, generally speaking, a job for shadows. As usual, you first have to decide from which direction the light is shining. Use the side of your pencil to draw the shaded part, and quit before you think you have to.

← It helps to have a very soft edge to the shadow.

Apple

Suggestion Pile: An apple, a pumpkin, a soccer ball, a head of lettuce, a baseball, a crystal ball, a globe, an ostrich egg, a bowling ball, a balloon, a squash, a boulder, a planet, a coin, a plate, a pot, a pancake, a puddle, a doughnut, a hatbox.

Add gentle shading
to turn these circles
into bubbles. You might
want to add a few
bubbles of your own.

Now It's Time to Try a Few Silhouettes

A silhouette is a drawing that's all shape with no perspective. The edges alone have to tell your whole story, so pick something with a distinctive shape and have a "story" or essence in mind from the beginning (see the suggestion pile for ideas). A winter tree might start with "spindly." A witch's profile might be "all nose." A dog can be "scrawny," "roly-poly" or "speed." Learn to respect your accidents. Sometimes you can start with "scrawny" in mind, but end up with "scared." Don't question fate. There may be greater powers at work here than either of us can know.

Suggestion Pile: A lady with a baby carriage and baby, two cats wailing, a leafless tree, man in a tophat on a bicycle, man with an umbrella with holes or blown inside out, elephant with birds on its back, old bird's nest in a leafless tree, flying beetle, fat man on a frail chair, pointing dog, carved pumpkin, pitchfork in a hay pile, person imitating "Y," kids on a seesaw, man carrying a ladder.

The Zoo of Your  Imagination

The Great Steaming Blurge

In this book we're going to start our section on drawing living things with a bit on the drawing of animals. And we're going to start *that* bit with a page or two of fantasy animals.

Fantasy animals may not be very realistic in the way they look, but they can be quite realistic in the way they feel.

Don't do a lot of planning here. It can get in your way. Just toss up an idea like "bird-ish," "dragon-ish," "fish-ish," or "bug-ish," and then give it a good swat. If you let your pen and pencil do half of the thinking, you'll be amazed at the kind of work they can do.

The Hopeless Flopper

Thank goodness at least one of us is normal.

The Small
Hairy Gloob

The LARGE
Hairy Gloob
fills this space.

Aaaargh. ⟶

P.S. It's best to name
your animal **after**
you've drawn it.

For example: This is a

_____
(fill in the blank)

Lie down and
rest your feet.

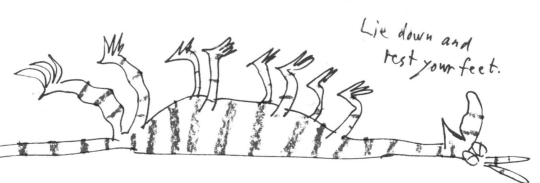

Lend Your Own Touch of Genius to These...

Finish up these drawings.

The Ten-legged Unexpected Thing.

The Nervous Furblow
(note the hysterical ears)

The Long-Tailed Werble

The Greater Spiked Glunk Falls in Love

The Greatly Feared 14-Legged Galumposaurus Needs a Back End

and some shoes...

...and socks...

and riders, of course...

....and SMOKE

Mrs. Thudkins Takes Her Floppaterasis for a Walk

I'm not going on to the page with _that_.

The 3-Headed Red-Spotted Gorff: A Triple Portrait

COME ALONG CUDDLIKINS

And Now It's Time for You to Learn a Little Bit About Dogs

tall and spotty

Simple ideas about dogs.

(You can supply the spots.)

Their back legs bend like this.

When they lie down their front legs often stretch out.

The legs fold like this.

When they sit down they are still standing up at the front.

When they are happy their tails and ears perk up.

And when they are unhappy, the opposite.

Dogs come in all
shapes and sizes.

For example:
        Large and hairy

(You can supply the
rest of the hair.)

Long and   low...

...Even longer and lower—

Give Free Rein to Your Dog  Imagination

Dogs, Dogs and Dogs

A page for you to do your own.

Birds

When it comes to drawings, it's the egg that comes before the chicken.

1. Draw an egg...

2. Add features!

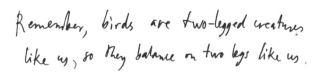

Remember, birds are two-legged creatures like us, so they balance on two legs like us.

Add Birds to This Page As Needed

Fantastic!

Wings can be UP

or DOWN

How to Draw a Pig

Like a bird, a pig is really just
an oval with features: curly tail,
four legs, big flat nose, no wings.

Basic Pig

Advice on the Pig

Start at the flat end.

go on to the curly end.

Pigs have trotters.

They're a bit like high-heeled shoes.

A pig from the front...

...has a friendly face.

Pigs also lie down and look happy.

A Pageful of Pigs

You add mama.

Horses ...

Big helpful hint: The back legs on a horse are a bit odd.
The front legs are straight enough. See below.

If you get the general sense of the way
a horse is arranged, you can add
more anatomy later.

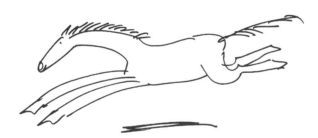

Before photography no-one knew what a horse's legs
did when it was running. So they drew them like this!
It's quite wrong, but it's still a good way to make
the horse look as though it's moving *fast*.

A Horse in Long Grass
solves a lot of problems

A Herd of Magnificent Horses (Yours)

Fishes, Fishes, Fishes  and Fishes

This is the basic fish shape

which has all kinds of variations ——

Fill in the fish blanks.

A Page in Need of Fish

(and seaweed too if you want to.)

Time for You to Do a Few Crocodiles ...

A crocodile is a sort of pointed log

A simplified crocodile

Go and take a look at a real crocodile
to see where the teeth really are

and Cockatoos ...

Add the cockatoo.

Home sweet Home!

Note the hairstyles.

A cockatoo tree—just add cockatoos!

Emotional Rabbits

Even a rabbit has feelings...

doubtful

sad

Enraged

Wistful

cheerful

Resolute

Attentive

Life out of doors

Pathetic

72

Your Turn

please finish the faces ... with *feeling* ...

And now—
some rabbits that are totally YOURS...
(don't forget the expressive ears).

Lunch

The Unspeakable Beauty  of the Human Face

A note of warning before you start: People (yourself included) pay an inordinate amount of attention to the human face (far more than is warranted, actually), and as a result they can be unreasonably picky about drawings of them. Consequently, you're into a sensitive area when you draw faces. Little lines make big differences and you will find yourself frequently unsatisfied with your efforts. Our recommendation? So what. Take a fearless experimental approach. Wield your pen or pencil with spirit and take bold chances. Your successes will shine all the brighter and the rest — nothing but necessary steps to greatness.

Right

Wrong

NOTE that the nose comes between the eyes and the mouth nearer the bottom of the face.

Eye ⟶
Nose ⟶
Mouth ⟶

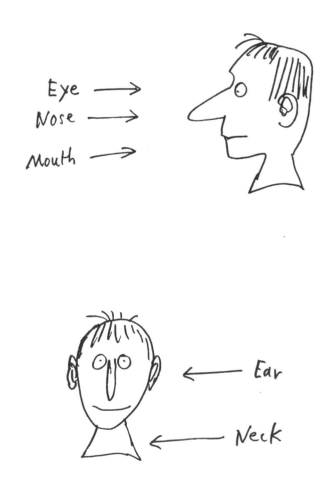

⟵ Ear

⟵ Neck

A Beginner's Page of Faces

She can balance an apple on her nose.

What amazing ears!

Her favorite animal is the giraffe.

He can hear what you say from miles away.

What an enormous nose!

Nothing escapes her gaze.

A Page on  Eyes

You may want to draw the eyes as dots ————

Or you may want to observe them from life. The soft pencil is better for this

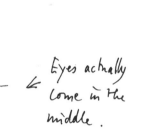

Eyes actually come in the middle.

If you experiment you may find you get some interesting effects with the soft pencil...

← But sometimes we like to draw them higher.

If you draw them as dots in circles — they can look to left or right.

← or sometimes lower.

Dealing with the  Hair

Heads also have hair.

It wants to grow UP

but it can't manage it for long.

Hair. Your Turn

Don't forget your red pencil.

Could you draw on something really exciting?

Now let your imagination run riot.

Noses, Ears, Necks.
Your Turn

Well that's a really fine neck.

Thank you I think your ears are great.

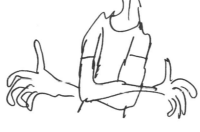

Don't forget the neck.

You certainly meet some strange characters round here.

You certainly do.

SMILE, PLEASE
and Other Expressions

Use everything you've learned to create a one-page gallery of rogues, saints, thieves, wise men (and women), fools, clowns, and charlatans.

What Happens When You Turn?

Your head shape changes. So does your nose and the place where the eyes go. It's tricky and you should expect to fumble at this. The simplest views are straight-ahead and profile. Below are some half-dones to start you off.

Hang These Pages with Incredibly Lifelike Portraits

PETS' CORNER

Dealing with Human Anatomy (OUR WAY)

The anatomy we show here is not right — but it's not wrong either. If you decide to add more detail later, you won't need to unlearn anything from these pages. And neither forget nor despair: Sins of botched details will all be forgiven if you can catch an essential bit of posture or gesture.

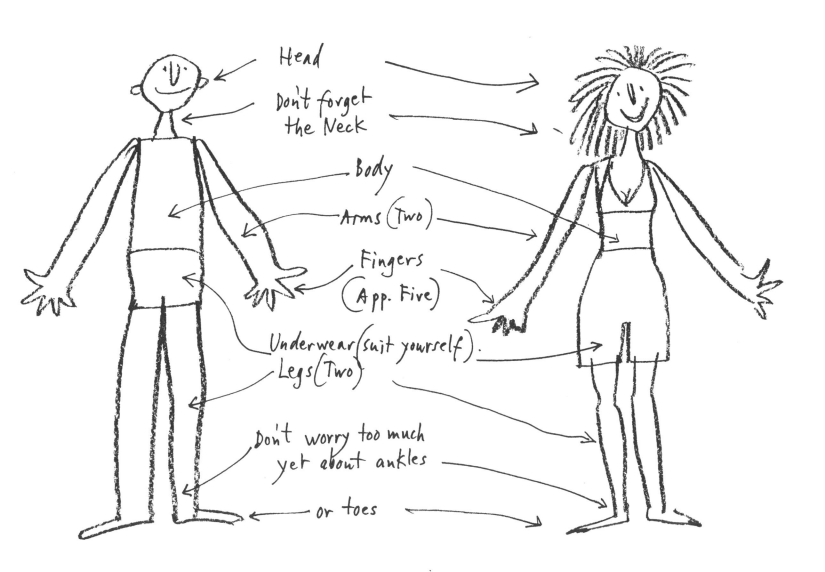

Head

Don't forget the Neck

Body

Arms (Two)

Fingers (App. Five)

Underwear (suit yourself).

Legs (Two)

Don't worry too much yet about ankles

or toes

Where Do the Arms Go?

Locating the arms can actually be a challenge since they point and move in so many different directions, some of which can be quite tricky to show. But at this stage in your career, take it easy on yourself. Draw figures in which the arms are out away from the body.

Having trouble getting your arms right? Don't worry! (as long as they join on.)

They went thataway.

Go to your room immediately!

Your Turn: Draw Some More Figures, Arms Out and Away from the Body

Man lifting safe.

Suggestion Pile: Hands in pockets, covering ears, pulling up pants, jumping jacks, fish story, attempting to fly, drawing bow and arrow, holding barbells.

Draw Some Figures with the Arms Crossing in Front of the Body

This is a far trickier task. Give yourself full points just for trying. And never try to draw someone with their arms crossed.

The Scratcher.

Don't worry if the drawing underneath shows through.

Thinks:

The Thinker.

Suggestion Pile: Hand covering face, pledge of allegiance, adjusting tie, buttoning shirt, hula, patting head/rubbing tummy, scratching belly indelicately.

Use These Two Pages to Draw More Figures

If you turn your figures just slightly to one side or the other, you can show a bit more character (or lack of it) in their backs. Someone shivering, for example, is hunched over. Someone stopping traffic has an authoritative uprightness to their posture. When you feel you're especially out of your depth, try the pencil and work lightly, making interesting mistakes with wild abandon. Then go back and darken lines that you want to.

Which of these arms do I like best?

Draw the person who is carrying this flowerpot on their head.

Draw the person who is carrying this bag of shopping.

The Difference Between Men and Women

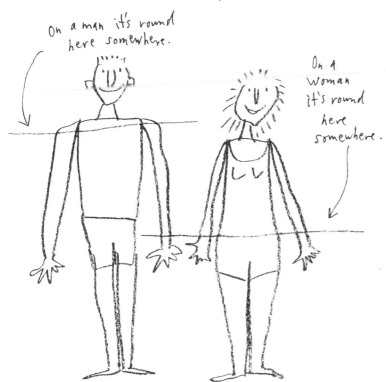

The Centre of Gravity

On a man it's round here somewhere.

On a woman it's round here somewhere.

Where's my centre of gravity?

I think it slipped.

Suggestion Pile: Draw a figure brushing teeth, shivering in cold, stopping traffic, biting nails, hands on head, rubbing eyes, pulling hair, hands on hips, scratching stomach.

89

Postures 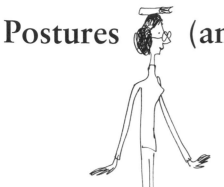 (and the Importance of Gesture)

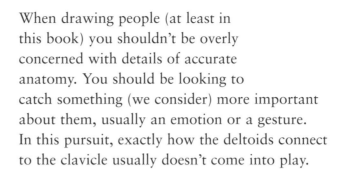

When drawing people (at least in this book) you shouldn't be overly concerned with details of accurate anatomy. You should be looking to catch something (we consider) more important about them, usually an emotion or a gesture. In this pursuit, exactly how the deltoids connect to the clavicle usually doesn't come into play.

This is not to say that you can stick an arm or a leg on anywhere you want (although that might be interesting from time to time). You just have to know what's important.

For example: Let's say you're drawing someone leaning over a short fountain. The key bit is that look of awkwardness. Someone pushing a stalled car has a stress in their posture. Get those essentials right, and you're free to botch the details.

A note of caution: Nailing down just the essential gesture or emotion is a bit like catching butterflies. There is some flailing. You'll miss a lot. But your reward will be startling and beautiful.

How to Catch Something Essential About Your People

This is a bit tricky and you will have to do a little more thinking and planning than we ordinarily suggest you need to do. The essential problem is that you, like other normal people, are probably unaware of where you put your hands when you're excited, or scared, or stumbling. You've never really looked at it.

So the task of drawing someone who is excited, scared or stumbling becomes a difficult visual memory problem. Add to that the need to determine which part of the posture or gesture is the essential part, and which parts are just details, and you are actually into the overlap area between drawing on paper and directing an actor on a stage. Our first suggestion: Give yourself a break and stand up before you start drawing and try to get into the pose yourself (or force someone else in the room to do it). Stare for a moment at the things you've never stared at before. Sometimes a little detail (the angle of an elbow?) can be the most telling bit.

In this drawing the red lines are the ones that suggest the movement.

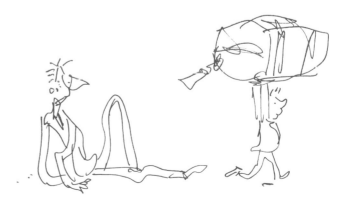

More Figures

The empty space on these two pages is all yours. Please fill it with a crowd of characters from your imagination. Around here we honor mistakes and botched details. Please make many.

Getting Your People to Balance

One of the "essentials" you'll be trying to capture in any figure is its sense of balance. People on two legs are always a little precarious, like bicyclists, and as you move an arm one way, or a leg, bear in mind the possible need to stretch the opposing limb in the opposite direction. Just for balance.

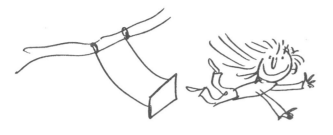

Getting Your People to *Fly*

Of course, if you want to forget all those difficulties with balance, just toss your people up in the air. Draw a little shadow under them, or perhaps a trampoline, and your problems with balance will go away.

Despite the fact that there are some (interesting?) problems with the size and proportions of this little girl, the essential point, the energy of the fling, is in there somewhere.

Try a Few More Fliers Here

Trampoline Artist
(note the hair)

Getting Your People to Sit Down

Advanced work here, but that's what you have to expect when you're this far back in the book. Draw in profile (makes things a little easier) and begin with your sitter's back. Have a "look" in mind before you begin — crisp, slouching, snoozing... whatever.

Somehow he can't seem to get the idea of it

Probably Your Very First Procession

Finish all these drawings, not forgetting to use your red pencil. Sign your work when you're finished, please.

The three-legged
four-headed Nurgle

The giant
goofy daisy

The long-eared
Moon Rabbit

The Hairy Dog

Marvo the
Amazing
Balancing Act

Ermintrude
and her
Umbrella

Probably Your Very Second Procession

Finish all these drawings, not forgetting to use your red pencil. Sign your work when you're finished, please.

The Lady with
the Crazy Hat

Karen and
her balloons

The Lesser
Clumposaurus...

Do Not Allow This Page to Remain Blank

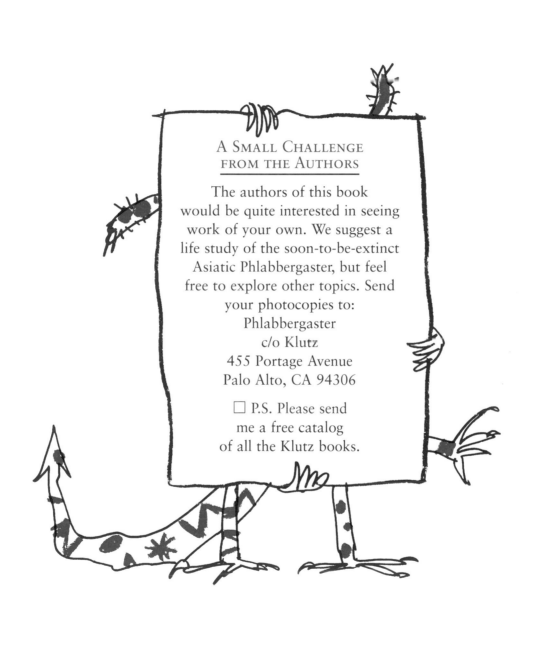

A Small Challenge
from the Authors

The authors of this book
would be quite interested in seeing
work of your own. We suggest a
life study of the soon-to-be-extinct
Asiatic Phlabbergaster, but feel
free to explore other topics. Send
your photocopies to:
Phlabbergaster
c/o Klutz
455 Portage Avenue
Palo Alto, CA 94306

☐ P.S. Please send
me a free catalog
of all the Klutz books.

BOOK DESIGN AND
GRAPHIC PRODUCTION
Kevin Plottner

TEDIOUS INTERFERENCE
MaryEllen Podgorski

KLUTZ CATALOG!

You can order the entire library of 100% Klutz certified books, replacement pens and pencils, and a diverse collection of other things we happen to like, from The Klutz Catalog. It is, in all modesty, unlike any other catalog — and it's yours for the asking. Just give us a call, write us, or order it on our website.

KLUTZ.®
455 Portage Avenue
Palo Alto, CA 94306
(650) 424-0739

KLUTZ.com
Come on in! OPEN 24 HOURS

MORE GREAT BOOKS FROM KLUTZ

If you enjoyed *Drawing for the Artistically Undiscovered*, you might be just the type to appreciate *Watercolor for the Artistically Undiscovered* by Thacher Hurd & John Cassidy.

A Book of Artrageous Projects

Create Anything with Clay

Draw the Marvel Comics™ Super Heroes™

Painted Rocks

The Shrinky Dinks® Book

Window Art

DO YOU TEACH?

Would you be interested in a classroom set of build-your-own Klutz books? E-mail bookfactory@klutz.com, write, or visit our website for details.